CONTENTS

GENERAL LEARNING OBJECTIVES OF THIS UNIT

This Open Learning Unit will supply you with all the core information you need to answer an examination question or to write an essay on remembering and forgetting. It will take you three to four hours to work through, though if you attempt all the suggested activities, it might well take longer.

By the end of this Unit, you should:

 be familiar with the basic theories and explanations of memory, appreciate its limitations;

 and be able to apply this knowledge to practical situations like studying.

1 Remembering

KEY AIMS: By the end of Part 1 you will be able to:

▷ *Define memory*

▷ *Explain the three stages of memory*

▷ *Describe the three theoretical models of memory*

▷ *Explain the physiological basis of memory*

▷ *List eight strategies for improving your memory.*

What is Memory?

▶ What do the following activities all have in common:

riding a bicycle;
talking to a friend;
meeting someone you haven't seen for years;
going to the bathroom?

▷ They would all be impossible without *memory**. It is memory that allows you to learn from and make sense of all your life experiences. Without it, everyone would be a stranger to you; conversations would be impossible; motor skills would have to be mastered anew every day and your family would get tired of telling you where the bathroom was!

▶ So how can one define memory?

▷ A simple working definition might be that it is *the retention of experience or learning.*

EG: *Have you ever experienced that awful feeling when you are in an exam, or part way through a conversation, and your mind goes completely blank?*

EG: *Try to imagine the frustration of the woman who has suffered a stroke and who can see faces and describe them accurately while looking at them, yet who cannot put a name to any face. When she walks through the streets of her home village she can never meet anyone she knows.*

EG: *Have you ever bumped into someone you haven't seen for years, and yet the mere sight of them brings all sorts of memories of your shared past flooding back?*

These examples demonstrate types of memory success or failure.

The cognitive approach

Psychologists look at memory in two ways. Cognitive psychologists are concerned with how the process of memory can be explained; while neuro-psychologists are interested in how and where the information is stored in our brains.

SOMETHING TO TRY

Look up the telephone number of the first 'A. Smith' in your local directory. Put the directory away and then write the number down.

How did you perform this task?

ENCODING — First, having found A. Smith, you had to put the relevant
↓   numbers into your memory system.
STORAGE — Then you had to keep them in your memory long enough to be
↓   able to
RETRIEVAL — recall them on to paper.

Encoding*, storage* and retrieval* are the three processes of memory. A failure at any stage will lead to forgetting.

If you were asked to write down A. Smith's phone number again now, without referring back to the original, you probably could not do it, and yet you could write down your own telephone number. Why is this?

It seems that there must be more than one type of memory. The most common distinctions you will come across are between:

> sensory register*
>
> short-term memory*   and
>
> long-term memory*

Sensory register

This is so-called because it refers to a fleeting memory which is registered by the sensory receptors of sight (iconic memory) and sound (echoic memory).

Iconic memory* Sperling (1960) showed individuals a screen on which three rows of three letters were displayed for only 0.05 of a second. After the nine letters disappeared from the screen the participants could only recall about half of them.

But, more interestingly, if participants were asked to recall a particular row of three letters immediately after the letters disappeared, by means of a tone cue (high for top row, low for bottom row etc.) they could do so almost perfectly.

K	Z	P
T	B	W
L	N	S

FIGURE 1.
Letter matrix similar to that used by Sperling, 1960.

If, however, Sperling delayed recall by as much as a second, the iconic memory was lost and participants' recall was reduced to only one or two letters in any line.

How can this be explained?

It certainly seems that all nine letters must have been available for recall momentarily, but *only* momentarily. This fleeting photographic memory is called iconic memory (i.e. picture memory).

Echoic memory* We have a similar sensory memory for sound called echoic memory. This seems to last about three or four seconds.

EG: *In conversation with someone you may miss part of what is said and you ask them to repeat it. Then before they say anything you seem to hear in your mind an echo of what was said.*

Short-term and long-term memory

For most of our lives we succeed in holding on to information for longer than an icon or echo can last. Remembering A. Smith's telephone number, or where the car is parked, clearly involves more information capacity than a sensory register could hold. We must, therefore, have an additional memory system or systems.

Some information (phone numbers are a good example) is only retained for a brief period of, say, a minute. Our memory for these relatively recent items is often called short-term memory (STM).

On the other hand, some material is stored for much longer periods of time, perhaps up to a lifetime, and this is called long-term memory (LTM). LTM is involved in riding a bicycle, or remembering where you went on holiday five, ten or more years ago.

Consider why memory loss is so disabling. Which would be worse, loss of short- or long-term memory?

The three stages of memory

Earlier in this Unit, when you tried to remember a phone number long enough to dial it correctly, you learnt that the three stages of memory are encoding, storage and retrieval. We will look more closely at these stages now.

5

Encoding

Clearly we can remember nothing unless it has been put into our memory. This encoding, as psychologists call it, can be acoustic (for verbal items), visual (for nonverbal items such as places and faces) or semantic (for meaning).

We do not fully understand how an event (a smell or a sight, for example) is transformed into a code that is held in memory. There is, however, some link between encoding and perception* (the taking in and making sense of information) and also with attention*. The event may or may not be analysed or processed further, depending on whether or not you attend to it. In fact, many so-called memory problems are the result of failure to attend.

EG: *In a classroom your tutor is explaining a particularly complex theory, but you see a hot air balloon out of the window. It is unlikely that you'll be able to remember what your tutor wore, let alone what she said, but you will probably be able to describe the advertisement on the balloon. It is all a question of what you pay attention to.*

Acoustic coding tends to be used when we try to keep information active by rehearsing it in our head. Conrad (1964) provided evidence for acoustic coding. You can try this experiment on yourself.

SOMETHING TO TRY

Look at the following seven consonants for about 15 seconds:

    K L R B S H Z

Now cover the letters and write them out in order.

Did you get them all correct? You will have noticed that you rehearsed the information in your head. If you did not get them all right, it is likely that you made an error on letter B, perhaps writing G, T or D. This is because you encoded it as 'ee'. Sometimes part of the code is lost, but the 'ee' remains and 'gee', 'tee' or 'dee' are all consistent with what remains.

If you try the same procedure again with acoustically similar letters, such as

    B V P C G D T

you will find it much harder to recall the items in order.

Visual coding is not very useful for verbal material, but becomes more important for nonverbal items (faces, pictures etc.) that are difficult to rehearse acoustically.

Encoding meaning This is the dominant method for ensuring that material is put into long-term memory.

EG: *If you ask two people to memorize the following letters, in order:*

    R A E D Y A D H T R I B Y P P A H

but tell only one of them that the letters spell out 'Happy Birthday Dear', in reverse, and then about an hour later you ask them to write down the letters in their original order, the person who was told what the letters spelled out should have no difficulty achieving 100% success. The letters were given meaning.

Often items you need to recall are meaningful, but the connections between them are not. In this case you can create real or artificial links between the items. For example, you may already know the colours of the spectrum:

Red
Orange
Yellow
Green
Blue
Indigo
Violet

because of the sentence 'Richard Of York Gave Battle In Vain', which converts the first letter of each word of the sentence to provide the cue for the colour.

Encoding specificity principle* Sometimes we encode prompts (or cues) that help us to recall something. Actors learn their lines by encoding the end of another actor's words. This can be seen, for example, when one actor ends a speech or performs a particular action, and the next actor is cued to begin his or her words to follow on the dialogue.

Tulving and Thomson (1973) formulated the encoding specificity principle which states that:

> the cue will succeed in retrieving a memory trace if, and only if, the information contained in that cue is encoded in the memory trace.

This means that we encode not just the target words (or actions, in the acting example), but also the context in which the words occur. The closer the context in which retrieval takes place is to the time of encoding, the more likely it is that retrieval will be correct.

SAQ
1

Identify, with an example for each, two ways of encoding information.

Storage

Once we have encoded an item of information it has to be stored in memory. How is our capacity limited?

This is best illustrated by a simple experiment.

SOMETHING TO TRY

Write down seven random sequences of digits, beginning with four digits (e.g. 6251) then five digits (e.g. (82947) and so on and finishing with a sequence of ten digits (e.g. 8135294716). Then, one sequence at a time, recite them to a friend and ask him or her to write down each sequence immediately after you have finished saying it aloud. When all seven sequences have been tackled, compare your friend's sequences with your original ones. Note how many digits were remembered in the correct order.

You should find (and this would be confirmed if you repeated the experiment with a number of participants) that your friend could accurately repeat sequences of between six and nine digits. It is unlikely that a sequence of ten digits was repeated in the correct order.

As early as 1885, Ebbinghaus noted this limit on STM of around six or seven items of information when he began to study memory scientifically. However, George Miller's account in *The Magical Number Seven, Plus or Minus Two: Some limits on our capacity for processing information* (1956) is probably better known as a description of the limit of short-term memory span. In this, Miller extended the observation Ebbinghaus had made some 70 years earlier, making the range more precise.

Chunking* Miller shows how information can be chunked by using existing memory stores while encoding or categorizing new information in order to expand the limited storage capacity of STM.

SOMETHING TO TRY

Below are 25 items of information to be learned. Unfortunately, because 25 far exceeds seven plus or minus two you'll find them difficult to memorize ...

O	I	L	T	U
G	T	A	A	E
A	G	E	N	C
E	N	M	O	N
M	O	I	P	O

However, you can organize them into one chunk of information. If you begin reading at the bottom righthand corner of the square and drop to the bottom of each row in turn, you will find it reads:

   once upon a time, a long time ago.

This organization of information increases the storage capacity of STM *and* imposes meaning on otherwise unrelated letters/numbers and makes them more likely to be recalled.

It is generally believed that LTM has enormous storage capacity and thereby enables us to deal with the past and the present simultaneously (Landauer, 1986). It explains how you can be faced with a novel problem but be able to remember and use possible solutions from the past, at one and the same time.

▶ Is anything ever forgotten?

Some people think that our memory is like a dusty attic and that if we could somehow get into it, we would find all our past experiences stored in there, intact. Freud believed that memories were not destroyed, although they might be repressed.

However, although we may have an enormous LTM storage capacity, there is no suggestion that we store information as precisely as a video tape or a computer does. Much depends on how the information is encoded, stored and retrieved. Breakdowns or distortions in memory can occur at any of these three stages. (Forgetting is dealt with in more detail later in this Unit.)

Organization* If you go into the library to find a book on memory, you would look in the medical or psychology sections. If you were looking for a Shakespeare play, you would go to the drama section. Organizing the library in this way makes it easier for you to find what you want.

Memories are also organized on the basis of meaningful information.

EG: *Name a make of car that begins with* V.

▶ What do you have to do to perform this task?

Clearly, to find something to fit the categories identified, you do not systematically search through your entire database of all kinds of information to get the right answer. You selectively search knowledge only about makes of car.

Organizing at the encoding and storage stages helps to ensure that information is sensibly arranged. You will, no doubt, regularly group, classify or categorize information to help you remember better in your preparation for tests or exams.

You often find that if people are given lists of items to remember, they will recall them in clusters, showing that they have used a degree of organization.

Tulving (1962) demonstrated this when he asked people to remember the same 16 randomly-chosen words over 16 trials, but each time presented them in a completely different order. Of course, recall improved on each trial, but Tulving was interested in the *order* in which words were remembered. Over successive trials the participants had a strong tendency to recall the items in recurring groups. Tulving suggested that his participants were imposing organization on the words in this task. By this he meant that the participants tried to group items in a way that made some kind of sense to them.

► Is there an optimum number of categories for organizing information?

▷ Interestingly enough, Mandler (1968) showed that seven seems to be the optimum number. You will remember that this is the same as the short-term memory span (Miller, 1956).

Organization can be aided by using language to link otherwise unrelated items. Bower and Clark (1969) found that students who were asked to make up a narrative story connecting 10 nouns were more successful at recalling them than students with the same study time who did not use any particular memory strategy.

EG: *If you had to learn the following list of words:*

vegetable	*basin*
instrument	*merchant*
college	*Queen*
carrot	*scale*
nail	*goat*

a narrative story, such as even this nonsensical one, might help you:

> *e.g.* A *vegetable* can be a useful *instrument* for a *college* student. A *carrot* can be a *nail* for your fence or *basin*. But a *merchant* of the *Queen* would *scale* the fence and feed the carrot to a *goat*.

Identify two different ways in which memory storage can be improved.

 A POSSIBLE PROJECT

1. *Create three lists of 10 concrete nouns.*

2. *Ask 10 participants to learn each list by making up a story to incorporate all of the words. (You may need to demonstrate this, perhaps by using the example given, to ensure that your participants understand the task.) Give this experimental group a time limit of two minutes to learn all three lists.*

3. *Also ask 10 control group participants to learn each list, in the two minutes time limit.*

4. *Test each participant* **immediately** *after they have learnt each list. (There should be no significant difference in the results between control and experimental groups at this stage.)*

5. *After all three lists have been presented, ask all participants to recall as many of the 30 words as possible. (You should find the experimental group recall two to four times as many words as the control group.)*

The important thing to notice here is that good organizational strategies are not necessarily immediately beneficial; but at a later time their advantages can be enormous.

Retrieval

Retrieval refers to the way you locate and access information that has been stored in memory. There are many different types of retrieval that can be measured experimentally.

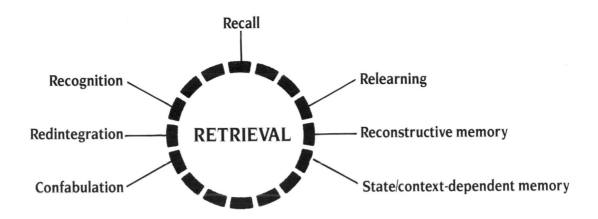

FIGURE 2. *Different forms of retrieval.*

(a) *Recognition** — is when something or somebody seems familiar whether or not you are able to name or identify them.

(b) *Recall** — is when you may well have few or no cues to help retrieval and you have to search your memory actively for something you learned at an earlier time. Timed essays require this type of retrieval.

(c) *Relearning** — when you haven't spoken French for 10 years and then have to use it on holiday, with a phrase book, it seems much easier to learn a second time round than it was originally.

(d) *Redintegration** — justifies all the souvenirs you buy!

EG: *When you look at the stuffed donkey you brought back from Spain, you begin to search your mind until you have a coherent memory of your holiday in Benidorm. The memory search can be fairly systematic, but other associated memories may 'pop' into your consciousness.*

(e) *Reconstructive memory** — is the memory involved when you pass information to someone else. This kind of remembering is involved in eyewitness testimony. You may unintentionally distort the objective truth, as you interpret it in the light of your own beliefs, schemas, stereotypes, expectations, etc. This is the memory involved in gossiping or spreading rumours.

(f) *Confabulation** — refers to a memory error that is often made when you are highly motivated or aroused. You fail to remember a particular detail so you invent something that seems likely.

EG: *People asked to give an account of a particular birthday, which is usually a happy, exciting or otherwise memorable event, often create a version which turns out to be the combination of several birthdays.*

(g) *State- or context-dependent memory** — if you learn something in one state (happy or drunk) or one particular place or context (say in classroom 4) and are then asked to recall it in another state (sad, sober) or context (the exam room) you will be less successful than if the state or context matched on both occasions. This means that if you are reading this Unit in a comfortable armchair in a warm room, when you are feeling particularly cheerful, you are more likely to remember it in that same situation, than in a cold exam room, sitting on a hard chair, when you are feeling anxious. Unfortunately, examiners do not take this into account!

SAQ
3

As you walk down the street you meet a friend you haven't seen for some time. In the course of your conversation you show her your holiday photos and tell her about a mutual friend who is rumoured to be having an affair with her boss. You reminisce over the last party you attended together.

Which types of retrieval were responsible for the memories you shared?

Checklist

1. Memory is the retention of experience or learning.

2. There are three processes involved in memory: encoding, storage and retrieval.

3. Encoding is the term given to putting information into memory. It may be acoustic (such as when we rehearse information in our head), visual (useful for nonverbal items such as faces) or for meaning.

4. Storage has a limited capacity of 7 $\pm$ 2. Organization and chunking can help to maximize the storage capacity.

5. Retrieval refers to the location and accessing of information stored in memory. There are several different forms of retrieval: recognition, recall, relearning, redintegration, reconstructive memory, confabulation and state- or context-dependent memory.

6. There are different types of memory. The most common distinctions are made between sensory register, short-term memory and long-term memory.

7. The sensory register refers to a fleeting memory registered by the sensory receptors of sight (iconic memory) and sound (echoic memory).

8. Short-term memory is the memory for relatively recent items, whereas long-term memory may hold information for up to a lifetime.

Models of memory

When psychologists are trying to explain a theoretical idea they often use models*. These are often diagrammatic representations of what are usually complex processes. Models help us to make predictions about behaviour and help generate hypotheses for further research.

As our understanding progresses we sometimes reject one model in favour of another, or modify it in the light of new findings. This is the case with the three models of memory:

1. The two-process (dual-memory or structural) model*
2. The levels of processing (depths of processing or process) model*
3. The working memory model*

The two-process model (Atkinson and Shiffrin, 1968; 1971)

The two processes referred to in the name of this model are STM and LTM. According to this model, incoming information is received by one of the sensory registers and, if it is attended to, it passes into STM. If not, the information is lost.

All that passes into STM may be rehearsed and transferred into LTM, or retained in STM as long as it is required. Rehearsal* is the repetition, usually subvocal ('said in the head'), of what has to be memorized. Enough rehearsal will result in information being transferred into LTM. However, information in STM may be displaced by new items as STM reaches its capacity of 7 $\pm$ 2.

Once an item is in LTM, interference* or decay may cause the item to be lost.

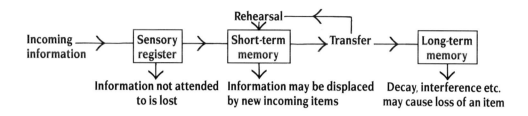

FIGURE 3. *Atkinson and Shiffrin's two-process model of memory.*

Evidence to support the two-process model

Free recall experiments

Free recall refers to an experimental procedure where participants are asked to remember a number of items in any order they choose (i.e. they do not have to recall them in the order in which they were presented).

If you ask people to recall 20 or more words, presented one at a time, they will usually recall more items from the end of the list. This is called the recency effect* (Murdock, 1962). They may also recall some words from the very beginning of the list — the primacy effect*. Interestingly enough, slower rates of presentation can improve the primacy effect, but have no influence on the recency effect.

The graph (see Figure 4) that shows primacy and recency effects is called a serial position curve* because it demonstrates the effect upon memory that relative position in a list will have.

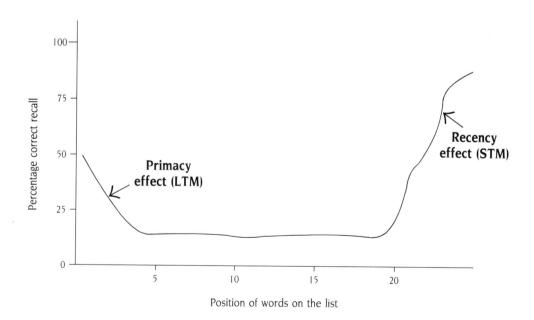

FIGURE 4. *A typical serial position curve.*

You might wish to try replicating Murdock's experiment, perhaps varying the rate of presentation, to see if you get a similar recall curve.

How does this curve support the two-process model?

The first words presented entered STM where there was little other material and so they were likely to be rehearsed and transferred to LTM. As more words were presented, STM filled up and there was no chance to rehearse or transfer later words to LTM. So the primacy effect suggests recall from LTM.

The recency effect can be explained by the fact that the words which were recalled first were the last words to enter STM and were not displaced by further items.

The Brown-Peterson technique

If you ask people to count backwards in threes (i.e. 60, 57, 54 etc.), after hearing a short series of consonants grouped in threes (such as DVJ, HTP, BGR etc), 90% of material is forgotten if recall is delayed by as little as 15 to 20 seconds. (The counting backwards interferes with rehearsal, and so limits the amount of material which can be kept in STM.)

The 10% that is recalled is thought to have been transferred to LTM (Brown, 1958; Peterson and Peterson, 1959).

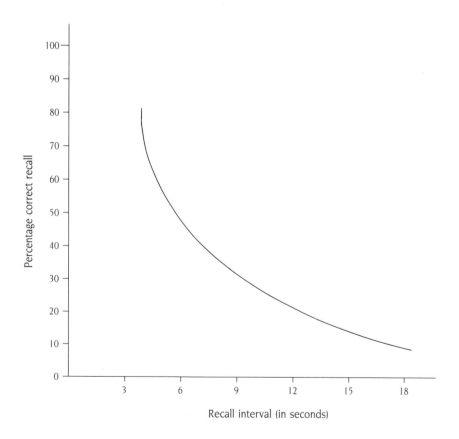

FIGURE 5. *The effect of an interference task on recall.*

The central weakness of the two-process model is that it implies STM is needed for transfer to LTM. It also assumes that information in the sensory registers (the first of the stores) is in a relatively raw and uninterpreted form, whereas in STM it will be coded by sound (due to rehearsal), and in LTM it will be encoded semantically. What the model fails to consider is how the information dramatically changes in nature.

Generally this model is seen as too rigid and simplistic. Although the distinction between short-term and long-term memory stores is a valid one, the cognitive processes are much more complex than this allows for.

In your own words, explain the two-process model of memory.

Levels of processing model

Craik and Watkins (1973) noted two different types of rehearsal:

(a) *maintenance (rote) rehearsal** (simply repeating the material in its original form as you do with a phone number, or your times tables)

(b) *elaborative rehearsal** (this involves a search for meaning or association, which is how you commit examination work to memory because the questions you will be asked at this level are not likely to draw on rote learning, but on your understanding).

Exactly how we 'rehearse' information, what we 'do' to it, or how we 'process' it to ensure that we remember it is clearly crucial.

Concentrating on the nature of the rehearsal (or processing) Craik and Lockhart (1972) proposed a second model of memory suggesting that how long the memory lasts is directly related to the level of processing, not simply the amount of rehearsal, and this explains why some items are remembered and others lost. Three levels of processing are identified:

(i) Structural level — What does it *look* like?

(ii) Phonetic level — What does it *sound* like?

(iii) Semantic level — What does it *mean*?

These move from the shallowest level of analysis to the deepest level, since to understand meaning requires you to know what a word looks and sounds like before you can process meaning.

Which levels of processing do you use when you read the following statements?

(a) 'Bee' does not rhyme with 'cat'.

(b) 'Similar' and 'different' are opposite in meaning.

(c) 'DOG' is written in capital letters.

(d) 'How', 'cow', 'now' all rhyme.

(e) What fills the space: The man ate the _____ (apple/telephone)?

SOMETHING TO TRY

You can see whether there is any support for the levels of processing model by working through the words below. Try to work through one word every five seconds. The instructions are in brackets after each word. (For example, 'TREE (rhyme)', means 'think of a word that rhymes with tree' (bee, perhaps). 'TREE (adjective)' is asking you to think of a relevant descriptive word (such as leafy).)

CAR	*(adjective)*
BEECH	*(rhyme)*
SKY	*(rhyme)*
RABBIT	*(adjective)*
CAKE	*(rhyme)*
JACKET	*(rhyme)*
PENCIL	*(adjective)*
INK	*(rhyme)*
TENNIS	*(adjective)*
TROUT	*(adjective)*
GIRL	*(rhyme)*
COMPUTER	*(adjective)*
SIGHT	*(rhyme)*
CLOCK	*(rhyme)*
COW	*(adjective)*
BOOK	*(rhyme)*
VILLAIN	*(adjective)*
BED	*(adjective)*
HOUR	*(rhyme)*
MONKEY	*(adjective)*

Now cover up the page and write down as many of the original words as you can remember, in any order you like.

Next, see how many items were words you had found rhymes for, and how many you had used adjectives to describe.

SAQ 6

Which task (thinking of a rhyme or thinking of an adjective) should help you to remember better according to Craik and Lockhart's model?

Limitations of the levels of processing model

Baddeley (1974) has criticized this model for several reasons.

(a) It is rather vague and untestable.

(b) It seems to be saying merely that if an event has meaning it will be remembered, which should seem obvious.

(c) Most importantly, if percentage of recall (or recognition) is the only way of independently measuring level of processing, then the definition of level becomes circular, since any material that is recalled is described as deeply processed.

So perhaps it is more helpful to think of STM not as a separate memory store, but as a holding area where experiences or material can be held while they are sorted, organized or otherwise related to items already stored in memory. This leads us directly to the third model of memory, the working memory model.

The working memory model

Baddeley and Hitch's (1974) model attempts to overcome some of the problems associated with the earlier memory models which had short-term and long-term stores. One of the greatest limitations to other models of STM was the notion that items had to be coded phonologically (by sound, albeit subvocal) due to rehearsal, whereas we know that STM can handle visual information, too.

Baddeley and Hitch showed that participants given a short-term memory load concurrently with new items to retain in the longer term were much less affected by this load than would be predicted by the Atkinson and Shiffrin theory. This led Baddeley and Hitch to replace the idea of a passive short-term store with an active working memory system.

The working memory model replaces the idea of a short-term memory store with a *central executive* (a central processor for information) which is not restricted to one particular mode. This system can be viewed as hierarchical with the central executive controlling or directing the other components. The central executive is thought to be used when dealing with the most cognitively demanding tasks. It is a flexible system that can process information received by all the senses, in a variety of different ways. It can also store information over brief periods of time.

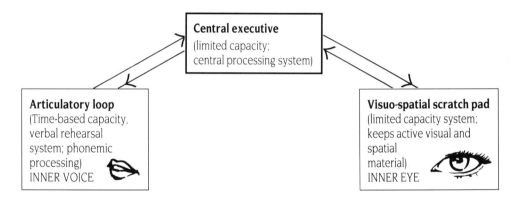

FIGURE 6. *The working memory model.*

The *articulatory loop* is a verbal rehearsal loop. When you try to remember a phone number for a few seconds by muttering it aloud (or subvocally) you are using the articulatory loop. It organizes information in a temporal and serial manner. (Temporal means in a chronological sequence, and serial means that items are in their presentation order.) It can be thought of as the inner voice. It seems to be used to supplement the storage capacity of the central executive on a somewhat limited range of tasks.

The *visuo-spatial scratch pad* can best be imagined as a rough note pad (in fact, in America, a notebook is called a scratch pad). It can hold more than one stimulus at a time and can rehearse information, but it deals with visual and/or spatial information rather than phonetic information. When you are walking along a familiar road and you think about the appearance and position of the pub just around the corner, this is an example of using the visuo-spatial scratch pad. It can be thought of as the inner eye looking over recorded information.

This model explains how drivers keep the memory of a warning road sign, even though there is no need for immediate action. It may be that after some time they accelerate, if there is no sign of the hazard; or perhaps they are ready to brake if, say, a deer crosses the road.

17

SAQ
7

Which components of the working memory system do you think would be involved in the following tasks:

(a) remembering a telephone number;

(b) listening to someone describing how to get from A to B;

(c) listening to a story?

▶ Is Baddeley's model, being the most recent, the best one to adopt?

▷ It is not enough to assume that Baddeley's model must be correct because it is the most recent. However, there is no doubt that the assumption that there are several different processing systems is more realistic than earlier ideas of a single, short-term store.

As it is technically quite difficult to design experiments that can tap the functions of the central executive (partly because its functions are likely to be highly integrative) most supporting experimental work has been on the articulatory loop and the visuo-spatial scratch pad (for example Baddeley, 1986; Morris and Jones, 1987; Logie, 1986).

The idea that short-term storage and attention are so closely related that they should be considered together at a theoretical level seems a sound idea, as is the notion that common processing resources are used in the performance of what appears to be a variety of cognitive tasks.

On the more negative side, the nature of the central executive is difficult to clarify. For example, it has been claimed that its capacity is limited, but no one has been able to measure the capacity. Also the claim that it is modality free (that is, not restricted to one mode of processing information) needs to be investigated in order to determine the exact limits on its functioning.

Lastly, the distinctions between the components of the model need clarifying. It seems likely that some phonetic processing can take place within the central executive, and perhaps also in an acoustic store, which may be an additional component or an aspect of the existing model, so it is hard to know how we can distinguish between the various components of the model.

Certainly the other models of memory have been investigated and found to be lacking, and so Baddeley's model represents our current state of thinking about STM, although it does not invalidate some of memory's observed features, such as the STM limit of 7.

We use models to help us understand rather complex processes, and to direct our attention to useful areas for research that will either confirm or contradict what the model suggests is going on. The working memory model is certainly generating experimental support (see, for example, Baddeley *et al.*, (1984); Morris and Jones, 1990).

Only further research will advance our understanding in the very complex area of memory. In a small way, your own experimental investigations are part of this advancement.

The neuropsychological approach

Neuropsychologists have looked for the physiological basis of memory in the brain: the how and where memories are located.

Lashley (1950) cut pieces out of rats' cortices after they had been trained to run a maze. No matter what part of the cortex he removed the rats kept at least a partial memory of how to solve the maze problem. It would seem, then, that memory does not reside in specific parts of the brain. It may be, of course, that memory resides in a number of locations within the cortex or outside it completely.

Gerard (1953) thought that memory lay in the electrical activity of the brain, so he trained hamsters to turn in a particular direction to obtain food and then lowered their body temperature until all electrical activity ceased. When the hamsters were revived and electrical activity began again they could still remember which direction to turn, hence disproving his view.

Patients who have lost their memories (amnesics) provide new information concerning the physical basis of memory. Typically, amnesics have suffered damage to the hippocampus*, temporal lobes* or the amygdala*. These are areas deep in the brain and are involved in processing declarative memories (facts that are easily learned and easily forgotten such as names, images or events).

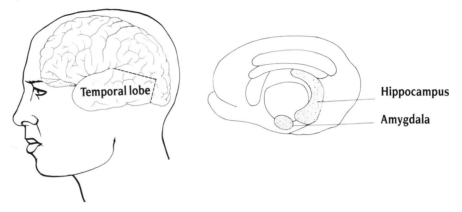

FIGURE 7a. *External surface of the left cerebral hemisphere.*   FIGURE 7b. *Cross-section of the brain.*

Because the memories of these patients prior to injury remain intact, it appears that the hippocampus and amygdala may be the places where *new* information is processed and directed on to other neural circuits (Mishkin and Appenzeller, 1987).

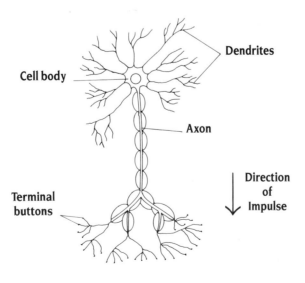

FIGURE 8. *A typical neuron.*

Some researchers are studying changes in and between single neurons. Since it is known that ECT* (electroconvulsive therapy) or a blow to the head can wipe out recent memories, but not affect earlier memories, it is assumed that chemical messages travelling through the brain circuits somehow eventually become consolidated into permanent neural change. The most likely place for this change to occur is at the synapses, where one cell communicates with another through a chemical messenger, a neurotransmitter*.

19

Although no two neurons are identical, most work in essentially the same way. The dendrites receive incoming signals from neighbouring neurons and the axon carries the signals received by the dendrites to other neurons. The signal is passed when a neurotransmitter is released across the synaptic cleft.

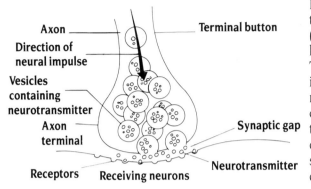

FIGURE 9. *The synapse.*

Kandel and Schwartz (1982), through studying the sea snail (Aplysia), have helped to shed light on how memory works. Their work pinpointed an increase in the secretion of a neurotransmitter when learning occurred, and when neuro-transmitters were blocked by drugs (alcohol, for example), the storage of information was disrupted.

Although the indications are that certain memories are stored in specific locations and that the processing of each type involves the activity of a complex neural system, it is clear that there is still a great deal to be discovered about the physical basis of memory.

SAQ
8

Explain what happens at the neuronal level when information is being put into memory.

?

What might be the advantages or disadvantages in having memories stored in specific locations?

Checklist

1. Three models of memory have been formulated: the two-process model; the levels of processing model and the working memory model.

2. The two-process model focuses on the transfer of information from STM into LTM, by means of rehearsal.

3. Free recall experiments and the Brown-Peterson technique support the two process model.

4. The levels of processing model derives from the different types of rehearsal. Elaborative rehearsal (as opposed to maintenance rehearsal) involves a search for meaning. The model suggests that there are three levels of processing: structural level; phonetic level and semantic level.

5. The working memory model attempts to explain how STM can handle visual material and concentrates on the active nature of the short-term store.

6. Neurologists have looked for where and how memories are located in the brain.

7. Areas of the brain such as the amygdala, hippocampus and temporal lobes appear to be especially important for memory.

8. Neurotransmitters (the body's chemical messengers) seem also to be implicated in memory, but our understanding of the physiological basis of memory is limited at present.

Implications and applications

▶ Can you remember how to improve STM?

▷ Enlarge the size of each chunk of information, since STM capacity is limited to 7 ± 2 chunks.

1 4 9 1 6 2 5 3 6 4 9 6 4 8 1 1 0 0 1 2 1 1 4 4

can be reduced to one chunk — the squares of the numbers 1 to 12 inclusive.

Some digit strings can be grouped into significant dates, or times, as in the case of 'SF' who, because he was an athlete himself, could recall 80 random digits by organizing each series of four digits into running times (such as 58.35, meaning 58 minutes and 35 seconds) (Ericsson *et al.*, 1980).

▶ *How can the study of memory increase your success as a student?*

Mnemonics

To improve LTM you can make use of mnemonic devices*. These are ways of assisting memory by using artificial devices, many of which depend for their success on visual imagery at the encoding stage. If you establish a meaningful connection between a word and an image (or between two words by means of an image) then this serves as a retrieval path.

There are several well-known mnemonic systems:

● Method of loci
● Numeric pegword system ('pigeonhole technique')
● Keyword method
● Narrative link
● Rhymes and rhythms

Method of loci Think of a list of items you need to buy from the shops. Then, using familiar locations, such as the rooms in your own home, form a visual image (taking at least five seconds) of each item linking it with a particular location.

EG: *In order to remember: bread, lipstick, dog food, and cheese, you could imagine your bedroom door with a slice of bread nailed to it; the bathroom mirror with a lipstick smile painted on it; the dog eating its food out of a sink.*

When you wish to recall the items, you simply have to take a mental walk, engaging your mind's eye, through the familiar locations.

Numeric pegword system Suppose you have ten items to remember. You begin by learning a simple rhyme.

one is a bun	six — sticks
two — shoe	seven — heaven
three — tree	eight — gate
four — door	nine — wine
five — hive	ten — hen

Then you picture the items to be remembered in association with the relevant pegword. For example, if you have to remember that the first word is 'sugar' you could visualize a bun piled over with sugar.

Keyword method   This is a good way to learn foreign vocabulary, amongst other things.

EG: *The Spanish word for 'horse' is 'caballo', which is pronounced 'cab-eye-yo'. 'Eye' becomes the keyword. You then form an image of, say, a horse kicking a giant eye and so establish a meaningful connection between the Spanish and English words.*

The keyword acts as a retrieval cue from Spanish to English and English to Spanish.

Narrative link   One disadvantage of the numeric pegword system is that you have to learn the 'one is a bun' rhyme at the beginning, and this takes time. The narrative link method (described earlier in the Unit) involves linking otherwise unrelated words, such as a list of things to be done in town, into a story. In the following example, the words in capitals are the words to be remembered.

EG: **"***Today I must be PRESENT at the LIBRARY when the CONCERT TICKETS are given out. If I FILE PAPER in the FOLDERS on the MAGAZINE stand, my EYE SHADOW will stay MILK-white. I will have to take care my TIGHTS are not damaged by the BIROS.* **"**

Rhymes and rhythms   You probably learned the rhyme 'Thirty days hath September ...' to help you work out the number of days in any month. You can buy tapes that teach children their times tables to pop music. These are both examples of how rhymes and rhythms can improve memory.

Other memory aids

In addition to mnemonic techniques there are other strategies to enhance memory such as:

- context re-creation
- organization
- PQRST method

Context re-creation*   When someone asks you what you were doing at 2pm on the 3 August 1989, you might feel like responding 'Don't be ridiculous. How should I know?'.

In fact, when you begin to re-create the context, you can remember a surprising amount.

EG: **"**3 *August — I was on holiday in Brittany. We stayed at a campsite in Carnac. It was the Thursday of our first week. We went to the beach in the morning and returned home for lunch at about 1.30pm so I must have been sitting down to bread, cheese, salad, fruit and wine.* **"**

You can't be sure that you actually remember all this. It may be inference, but it is probably close to the right answer.

Organization   You will remember from earlier in this Unit that organization during encoding improves subsequent retrieval. This principle is especially helpful when we need to store a massive amount of information.

Figure 10 shows a hierarchical organization to assist with revision of the topic Memory.

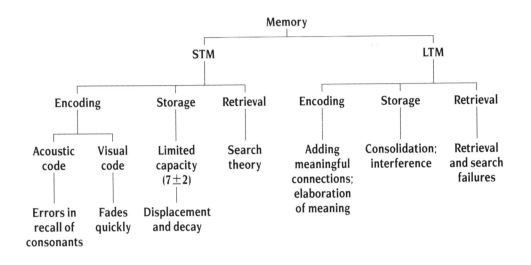

FIGURE 10. *Hierarchical organization of the topic Memory.*

PQRST method* The PQRST method is intended to help you improve your ability to study and remember material from textbooks. The initials in the name come from the five stages the method involved:

> **P**review
>
> **Q**uestion
>
> **R**ead
>
> **S**elf-recitation
>
> **T**est

Preview means skimming a chapter to identify main sections and subsections.

Question involves reading section/subsection headings carefully and turning them into questions.

You would then *read* the section to provide answers to the questions you created.

Self-recitation involves recalling the main ideas aloud (if alone) or subvocally. Question and Read stages involve elaboration of material and Self-recitation requires you to practise retrieval.

You try to recall the main points (*Test*) after you have finished the entire chapter.

So the PQRST method relies on three basic principles for training memory: *organizing* material, *elaboration* of material and *practising* retrieval (Thomas and Robinson, 1982).

23

What devices or strategies would you use to:

(a) *remember a particular junior school teacher;*

(b) *memorize a shopping list of eight items;*

(c) *prepare for a timed essay on the topic Memory;*

(d) *research a topic from written material?*

What strategies do you employ to help you to remember lists or ideas? Why are your strategies effective?

Checklist

1. STM can be improved by chunking information.

2. Mnemonics are artificial devices (such as method of loci, numeric pegword system, keyword method, narrative link and rhymes and rhythms) to improve LTM.

3. Mnemonics depend for their success on visual imagery at the encoding stage.

4. Other strategies to improve memory include the PQRST study method, context re-creation and organization.

Forgetting

KEY AIMS: By the end of Part 2 you will be able to:

▷ Distinguish between availability and accessibility memory problems
▷ Illustrate clinical amnesia
▷ Discuss problems of eyewitness testimony.

No doubt you have experienced that powerless feeling in an exam, or at an interview, when a crucial piece of information seems to have disappeared. Despite using memory successfully time and time again, all of us experience occasions when it lets us down. Why?

Remember the three processes involved in memory — encoding, storage and retrieval? A failure at any one of these stages can lead to forgetting.

Available but not accessible!

We must also separate problems of *availability* from problems of *accessibility*. Clearly, if an item of information has not been encoded or stored in the first place, it cannot be available for retrieval later. Both availability and accessibility refer principally to LTM. Something may be available in the long-term store, but unless the appropriate cues are available it may not be accessible.

If you look at a typical forgetting curve (Figure 11) you can see that forgetting is rapid at first but then slows down gradually. The first loss can be put down to trace decay, but the alternative theory is that subsequent learning and experiences interfere with existing memories.

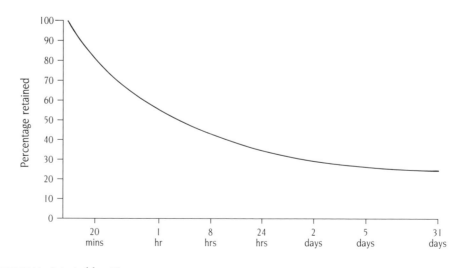

FIGURE 11. *A typical forgetting curve.*

25

The main theories of forgetting are illustrated in Figure 12.

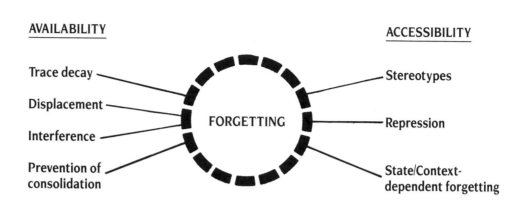

FIGURE 12. *The major theories of forgetting.*

Problems of availability

Trace decay* It is believed that learning leaves a trace in the brain as a result of excitation of nerve cells. There is a spontaneous weakening or fading of this memory trace as time passes, thus information may become no longer available. You will know from your own experience that forgetting increases with time.

According to Hebb (1949) trace decay can only apply to STM, as he believes that repeated neural activity causes a structural neural change, which would seem to correspond to LTM.

Other psychologists believe that there can be trace decay in LTM following the principle that if you don't use a skill, you lose it. Think how quickly you forget the vocabulary of a foreign language unless you practise regularly.

However, there is quite a powerful argument against the idea of trace decay in LTM, especially concerning motor skills. If you do not ride a bicycle for many years, you will probably find you still know how to despite having had no practice.

Waugh and Norman (1965) investigated trace decay in STM using a serial probe technique. They presented participants with sequences of 16 digits, at a rate of one to four a second. In testing recall, one digit is selected (the probe) and the participant's task is to name the digit that follows the probe. If trace decay occurs you would expect that participants would recall the digits more accurately if they were presented rapidly, as there would be less time between presentations and test. Waugh and Norman found no relationship between speed of presentation and recall, so this calls into question the validity of trace decay as the major source of forgetting in this task.

Displacement* Ask some friends to memorize the following list of digits. Allow about 20 seconds to present them orally:

6 9 1 5 3 8 7 1 6 2 4 3 7 8 2 9 4 6 5 9

How many did they remember? It should correspond roughly with seven, plus or minus two.

Because STM has a limited capacity, once it is full (with 7 ± 2 items), new information pushes out old information, which will no longer be available to memory. The memory trace of the new information will be strong compared with the older information which will have weaker traces.

Interference* It seems that the passage of time and the capacity of STM are not the only factors in forgetting. It may be that what takes place between learning and recall is also important in determining what is or is not available to be remembered. This leads to the additional theory of interference.

There are two kinds of interference:

● retroactive inhibition

● proactive inhibition

If you change your phone number, in a very short while you will find it hard to remember the old phone number. This is retroactive inhibition (RI) when new learning interferes with an existing memory.

In proactive inhibition (PI) the interference works forwards. For example, if you always park your car in a particular spot in a car park, and for some reason one day you are forced to park elsewhere, you may come out of work and be unable to remember where you parked the car. The memory of where you always park causes interference and forgetting.

Interference is quite easy to study experimentally.

A POSSIBLE PROJECT

1. *Devise two lists of paired associate words.*

   e.g. <u>List A</u>   <u>List B</u>
   dog — easy   *dog — rich*

   The first word (the stimulus) is the same for each list, but the second (the response) differs.

2. *Identify four groups of participants (2 experimental and 2 control groups). Or you could work with 2 groups if you wanted to study only RI or only PI.*

3. *Decide on standardized instructions.*

Procedure:

Retroactive inhibition (*recall of List* A *will be affected by the learning of List* B)

	Experimental Group	Control Group
Step 1	Learn A	Learn A
Step 2	Learn B	Rest
Step 3	Recall A	Recall A

Proactive inhibition (*the learning of List* A *will affect the recall of List* B)

	Experimental Group	Control Group
Step 1	Learn A	Rest
Step 2	Learn B	Learn B
Step 3	Recall B	Recall B

4. *If interference has been a factor in forgetting you should find a significant difference between each of the experimental and control groups in terms of their recall: i.e. Experimental Group 1 will recall less than Control Group 1, and Experimental Group 2 will recall less than Control Group 2.*

   It seems that PI increases with time while RI decreases over time.

The suggestion that the amount of forgetting of any particular set of information is an increasing function of the amount of similar material that has been learned in the past was well demonstrated by Crouse (1971). Participants were asked to learn a biographical passage about a fictitious poet John Payton and then learn two other biographical passages of a similar nature. When asked for details of Payton's life, participants were only able to recall 54% of the amount recalled by the control group participants who had been asked to read unrelated material after the biographical details of Payton.

Prevention of consolidation* Before a memory becomes firmly established in LTM a period of time is needed for the changes in the nervous system, which are a result of learning, to occur. Disruption during this time can result in the loss of the memory.

Trauma to the brain, including concussion, surgery or ECT can cause patients to forget events prior to the injury (retrograde amnesia), which would seem to support the idea that memories can be disrupted if they are not given time to consolidate.

Yarnell and Lynch (1970) questioned American footballers who had concussion immediately after their injury what play had preceded the concussion. The players could answer this question *immediately* after the concussion, but if asked again three to twenty minutes later, they were unable to recall the events.

This suggests that, although due to prevention of consolidation, the memories are no longer available, for a brief period of time they could have been accessed. This underlines the close link between availability and accessibility.

A number of researchers have looked at sleep as a possible time for the reorganization of learning experiences, perhaps during dreaming, but the results to date are disappointing. At best it appears that there is a slight tendency for dream sleep to be more helpful for memory consolidation than sleep without dreams (although some evidence contradicts this).

It is generally suggested that sleep helps consolidation rather than reorganization of experiences, as retention of memories can be disturbed if the learning is followed by a period where people are deprived of dream sleep.

Problems of accessibility

Stereotypes* Bartlett (1932) reported reconstructive distortions of a story, The War of the Ghosts, that he told to students and asked them to reproduce. The reproductions were naturally very shortened forms of the original but successive recountings of the tale omitted less and less. Bartlett also reported on how people's cultural background could determine which elements of the story will be repeated and this leads on to more recent work on stereotypes determining which memories are accessible to recall.

Snyder and Uranowitz (1978) tested whether people's stereotyped beliefs about homosexuals affected their access to memories of information already received. Participants read a 750-word passage about a woman named Betty. Subsequently some were told that Betty now lived as a lesbian, while others were told that she had a heterosexual life style.

In response to multiple-choice questions such as:

In high school did Betty;

(a) occasionally date men

(b) never go out with men

(c) go steady

(d) no information provided

students who were told Betty was a lesbian were more likely to recall (b) incorrectly (i.e. that she 'never went out with men'); those told she had a heterosexual lifestyle were likely to respond with (c). The correct answer was in fact (a) — she occasionally dated men.

If you are aware of what people already know and believe in relation to new information they are given, you can to some extent predict what they are likely to forget and also the direction and form of the memory distortions that will occur.

Repression* According to Sigmund Freud (1856-1939) some experiences are so painful that if they were allowed to enter consciousness, they would produce overwhelming anxiety. Instead, these experiences are repressed and stored in the unconscious, thereby becoming inaccessible. Repression is the ultimate failure to access memories because the target memories are actively blocked. Even when a person seems to be trying hard to recall a particular event, they will stop or digress when they come near to recalling the original, painful memory.

Repressive forgetting has several common features:

- the original experience has been encoded and stored by the individual, and recall can occur, sometimes spontaneously, sometimes as a result of hypnosis or 'free association'.
- recall cannot occur as a result of questioning or through conscious efforts to try to remember.

- repressed experiences always involve deep anxiety.

- repression is both active and continuous, involving constant and exhausting expenditure of energy. Sometimes the repressed event breaks through in a disguised form or perhaps during sleep. (If you have read or seen *Macbeth*, you will remember Lady Macbeth's sleepwalking scene when she tries to wash her hands to rid herself of the guilt of murdering Duncan.)

Exactly what is repressed varies from individual to individual. But always some extremely unpleasant emotional reaction (fear, guilt, sorrow, shame etc) is aroused when the event is recalled. The memory can only be retrieved when the emotional tension associated with it is released. This is called abreaction* and it is usually achieved during therapy.

Abreaction does not eliminate the cause of the conflict, but it does make way for further exploration of the repressed feelings and experiences. (This process is also called catharsis*, as if it were a kind of emotional cleansing.)

Experimental investigation of the phenomenon of repression is not feasible for ethical reasons, although some studies have involved exposing participants to mildly upsetting experiences and there has been some support for the repression hypothesis (Erdelyi, 1985).

There are many case studies of repression which will vividly illustrate the emotional blocking of recall, such as those cited by Freud in *Psychopathology of Everyday Life* or chapter eight of Morgan and Lovell's *The Psychology of Abnormal People*.

State/context-dependent forgetting As mentioned on page 11, the state or context of people at the time of acquisition of information can affect their ability to access the memory later. If the states match (i.e. they were drunk when they learned the material and are drunk when asked to recall it) then recall is improved.

Bower (1981) manipulated the mood of his participants by hypnosis and showed clearly how the match or mismatch at the time of learning and recall had a strong effect on the accessibility of memories (see Figure 13 below).

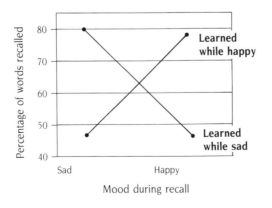

FIGURE 13. *A graph showing the effects of mood on memory.*

Unfortunately Bower's work has not been replicated, but researchers have shown that memory can be impaired by going from an alcohol to a non-alcohol state, or vice versa. Other studies have found similar results with marijuana and other drugs.

Zechmeister and Nyberg (1982) found that participants could imaginatively recreate the learning conditions and thereby reduce the effects of state-dependent forgetting.

Godden and Baddeley (1975) demonstrated context dependency with the learning of lists of unrelated words by deep-sea divers. Items learned on land were difficult to recall in the underwater environment. Similarly, words heard underwater may be forgotten once on dry land. Godden and Baddeley (1980) found no effect on recognition however.

*Explain the difference between availability and accessibility of information, and name at least **three** theories of forgetting that concern accessibility of material.*

Can you think of ways that exams, or other tests of your ability, could be presented which would help to eliminate some of these failures of memory?

Clinical amnesia

You are watching a film at the cinema. The hero tries to defend someone against the villains but he is knocked unconscious. When he regains consciousness his first words are often something like 'Where am I? Who are you?' and he can no longer remember the events immediately preceding the blow to his head. This is probably the most dramatic incidence of forgetting — clinical amnesia, which is the partial or total loss of memory.

Possible causes include:

- accidental damage to the brain
- stroke
- alcoholism
- ECT
- ageing and senile dementia
- encephalitis
- brain surgery (e.g. to reduce epilepsy)

Amnestic (or amnesic) syndrome* is the clinical term for the impairment of LTM where there is no deterioration of intellectual functioning nor any clouding of consciousness.

This syndrome is brought about by damage to either or both sides of the brain and some causes include chronic alcohol abuse and thiamine deficiency.

Anterograde amnesia* involves an impairment in the acquisition of new information, or in remembering day-to-day events. 'H.M.' is an extensively-studied case whose amnesia was the result of surgery to reduce epilepsy. He remembered everything he had learned before the surgery, but had severe problems remembering events following surgery. Although his STM was generally normal, he was either unable to transfer information into LTM, or unable to retrieve it.

Cases such as H.M.'s have been taken as additional evidence to support the two-process model of memory, since they clearly point to an STM/LTM distinction.

Psychogenic amnesia* is when some stressful episode suddenly results in a person being unable to recall important personal information. The general behaviour of the amnesic person is unremarkable apart from the loss of memory for all events during a limited period of time following the traumatic experience (such as rape), although sometimes the memory loss brings some disorientation.

31

Retrograde amnesia* is the inability to remember events that occurred prior to the injury or disease. This form of amnesia may last minutes, days or even years, although there is little or no disruption of STM. There is a consistent tendency for the forgotten period to shrink over time, but similarly consistent is the failure ever to recover the last few seconds prior to a head injury.

Some people (Freud, for example) have suggested that these few seconds are lost to a patient because they are so emotionally painful. Others have suggested that patients fail to take in the information from those last few minutes. However, Yarnell and Lynch's study of American football players mentioned earlier suggests that their memory for events prior to concussion had been available, but that lack of a consolidation period eliminated its availability.

These, and similar observations from other patients suffering accidental damage to the brain, further support the idea that a memory trace requires some time to be consolidated. A blow to the head can interfere with the physiological processes that lead to consolidation of memories, and hence, a permanent record of past events.

Some people suffering acute depression may be treated with ECT which involves an electric current passing through their brain inducing a cerebral seizure and temporary loss of consciousness. On recovering consciousness, patients are usually unable to recall events preceding the shock, in the same way that the patient who experienced head injury is unable to recall the moments just before the accident. And yet, in both cases memory for earlier events seems intact.

People in their 60s and beyond often suffer problems with their memory. This can be seen clearly when older people forget to pass on messages (or alternatively tell you the same thing several times), or more importantly, forget to take necessary medication.

This natural aspect of ageing should not be confused with senile dementia (or illnesses such as Alzheimer's disease and Huntingdon's chorea which exhibit similar symptoms). A serious decline in memory abilities is often the first area where difficulties are noticed in senile dementia, but this is followed by more general intellectual impairment.

The evidence supporting the notion that a deficiency of the neurotransmitter choline might be the key to halting the rate of decline of a demented person came from postmortem studies showing a deficiency of this chemical in the brains of those suffering senile dementia. Unfortunately, feeding quantities of choline to sufferers did not affect its concentrations in the brain. Once we know more about the neurochemistry of memory we may be able to slow down, or even halt, the problems of senile dementia.

Identify and describe three different causes of clinical amnesia.

What are the advantages and problems associated with studying memory defects from a clinical perspective?

Reconstructive memory and eyewitness testimony

Much of the experimental work undertaken in the area of memory has involved lists of words, and sometimes nonsense syllables. While this work can give us an insight into the workings of memory, we also need to look more at meaningful material and how it is remembered.

Memory, in common with perception, is constructive — if there are gaps in sequences or events, we tend to create missing information to fit in with other cues that are available. For example, given the following sentence: 'The bottle was broken during the pub brawl', we are likely to assume the bottle was a beer/wine/spirits bottle, not a milk bottle. Our general knowledge associates beer bottles rather than milk bottles with pubs.

Stress and memory As you will have already noted, stress can affect the ability to remember. Loftus and Burns (1982) showed participants a film of a hold-up and then tested their memory for details. The experimental group saw a violent version where one of a group of young boys is shot, and falls to the floor clutching his bleeding face. The control group did not see this scene; instead their film cut to a scene inside the bank where the manager is explaining to staff and customers exactly what has happened.

Participants who saw the violent version had less memory for details prior to the shooting, including the fact that one of the boys had a large number '17' on his jersey. Indeed, out of 16 items participants were asked to recall, those who had seen the violent version did worse on 14 of them. If you think that witnessing a real crime will inevitably be even more shocking, it is clear that information processing is bound to be adversely affected.

Weapon focus Loftus *et al.* (1987) have also shown that if a weapon is involved in a crime, the attention of witnesses is likely to focus on the weapon, and take in little else. This phenomenon has been called *weapon focus*.

Phrasing questions When you also consider that the way a question is phrased can affect a witness's response, reliability of eyewitness testimony has to be called into question. Loftus (1979) looked at the changing of the word 'the' to 'a' in the question 'Did you see the/a broken headlight?' to student eyewitnesses of filmed car accidents. In reality no broken headlight could be seen on the film, but 15% of the 'the' group said yes, compared to 7% of the 'a' group.

When Loftus changed the single word 'hit' to 'smashed' in the question 'About how fast were the cars going when they hit/smashed each other?' she found that 'hit' produced an average of 34 mph, but 'smashed' produced an average of 44 mph.

Hypnosis Sometimes eyewitnesses are unable consciously to recall information about a crime. Freud would probably have suggested that they had repressed unpleasant details. It is true that sometimes, under hypnosis, witnesses can recall accurately details they could not recall before. One reason might be that to imagine yourself back to the scene of a crime can help the recall process. Alternatively, if a memory has been repressed because of stressful associations, under hypnosis the memories may be brought to the surface.

It is wrong, however, to think of memory as a kind of videotape that can be rewound, frozen on a particular frame, or zoomed. Memory is not laid down in this way.

It should also be remembered that memories recalled under hypnosis are prone to the same problems as everyday memories — vague and incomplete recollections may become confabulated into a seemingly coherent memory.

Because evidence from witnesses who have been hypnotized is unreliable it is not admissible in court.

A POSSIBLE PROJECT

You will need at least one assistant to help you undertake a simple investigation into the reliability of eyewitnesses. You will also need access to a group of about 20 people, perhaps another teaching group.

First, you need to devise a strategy for a 'stranger' to enter a room containing a group of people for a brief period of time. The 'stranger' could take the regular tutor out of the room and you could ask the group to fill in two previously-prepared questionnaires asking for descriptions of the stranger and the tutor.

You could give prompts to aid recall (as the police would), such as height, weight, age, colour of hair, clothes worn etc.

A comparison of the accuracy of the descriptions of the familiar tutor and unfamiliar stranger should suggest how reliable/unreliable eyewitnesses can be.

Do you think it would be wise for courts to convict a person on eyewitness testimony alone?

The whole of this Unit has been written with you, the student, in mind, and your need to *encode, store* and *retrieve* information.

You should have noticed a logical organization to the Unit and the use of diagrams, things to try and SAQs which are all designed to help you to remember.

Some information has been elaborated to assist your memory. Sometimes imagery has been used. On other occasions you have been encouraged to rehearse (self-recite) material (through SAQs, for example).

You should become aware of which techniques work especially well for you so that you can apply them not only to other areas of psychology but to other courses you are following.

Remember, the benefits of any system may not be immediately apparent, but you will reap them in the long term.

ASSIGNMENTS

TUTOR ASSESSMENT

Please write one of the following essays to hand in to your tutor for marking. Spend no more than 45 minutes on the actual writing of the essay, although your planning and reading will take longer.

- ❏ Outline and evaluate the three psychological models of memory.
- ❏ Why, according to psychologists, do we forget?

If you have any difficulties with your chosen essay, please discuss them with your tutor.

ESSAY PLANS

To assist with your exam preparation, prepare essay plans for the following essay titles:

- ❏ Outline the strategies you could employ to help you remember verbal material more effectively.
- ❏ Describe, with supporting research evidence, how organization can assist recall of information.

FURTHER READING

BADDELEY, A.D. (1986) *Your Memory: A user's guide.* Harmondsworth: Penguin.

COHEN, G., EYSENCK, M. and LE VOI, M. (1986) *Memory: A cognitive approach.* Milton Keynes: Open University Press.

HOWE, M.J.A. (1983) *Introduction to the Psychology of Memory.* New York: Harper & Row.

For suggestions for experimental work on memory (especially eyewitness report):

BENNETT, A., HAUSFELD, S., REEVE, P.A. and SMITH, J. (1981) *Workshops in Cognitive Processes.* London: Routledge & Kegan Paul.

REFERENCES

Students studying psychology at pre-degree level, whether in schools, FE colleges or evening institutes, seldom have access to a well-stocked academic library; nor is it expected that they will have consulted all the original references. For most purposes, the books recommended in Further Reading will be adequate. This list is included for the use of those planning a full-scale project on this topic, and also for the sake of completeness.

ABERNATHY, E.M. (1940) The effect of changed environmental conditions upon the result of college examinations. *Journal of Psychology,* 10, 193-301.

ANDREOFF, G.R. and YARMEY, A.D. (1976) Bizarre imagery and associative learning: A confirmation. *Perceptual and Motor Skills,* 43, 142-148.

ATKINSON, R.C. and SHIFFRIN, R.M. (1968) Human memory: A proposed system and its control processes. In K.W. Spence and J.T. Spence (Eds.) *The Psychology of Learning and Motivation,* Vol. 2. New York: Academic Press.

ATKINSON, R.C. and SHIFFRIN, R.M. (1971) The control of short-term memory. *Scientific American,* 225, 82-90.

BADDELEY, A.D. (1976) *The Psychology of Memory.* New York: Harper & Row.

BADDELEY, A.D. and HITCH, G. (1974) Working memory. In G.H. Bower (Ed.)*The Psychology of Learning and Motivation,* Vol. 8. New York: Academic Press.

BARTLETT, F. (1932) *Remembering.* Cambridge: Cambridge University Press.

BOWER, G.H. (1981) Mood and memory. *American Psychologist,* 36, 129-148.

BOWER, G.H. and CLARK, M.C. (1969) Narrative stories as mediators of serial learning. *Psychonomic Science,* 14, 181-182.

BRANSFORD, J.D., FRANKS, J.J., MORRIS, C.D. and STEIN, B.S. (1979) Some general constraints on learning and memory research. In L.S. Cermak and F.I.M. Craik (Eds.) *Levels of Processing in Human Memory.* Hillsdale, NJ: Erlbaum.

BROWN, J. (1958) Some tests of the decay of immediate memory. *Quarterly Journal of Experimental Psychology,* 10, 12-21.

CONRAD, R. (1964) Acoustic confusion in immediate memory. *British Journal of Psychology,* 55, 75-84.

CRAIK, F.I.M. and LOCKHART, R.S. (1972) Levels of processing: A framework for memory research. *Journal of Verbal Learning and Verbal Behaviour,* 11, 671-684.

CRAIK, F.I.M. and WATKINS, M.J. (1973) The role of rehearsal in short-term memory. *Journal of Verbal Learning and Verbal Behaviour,* 12, 599-607.

CROUSE, J.H. (1971) Retroactive interference in reading prose materials. *Journal of Educational Psychology,* 43, 579-588.

ERDELYI, M.H. (1985) *Psychoanalysis: Freud's cognitive psychology.* New York: Freeman.

ERICSSON, K.A., CHASE, W.G. and FALOON, S. (1980) Acquisition of a memory skill. *Science,* 208, 1181-1182.

FREUD, S. (1914) *Pschopathology of Everday Life.* London: Allen & Unwin.

GERARD, R.W. (1953) What is memory? *Scientific American*, 118-126.

GLANZER, M. and CUNITZ, A.R. (1966) Two storage mechanisms in free recall. *Journal of Verbal Learning and Verbal Behaviour*, 5, 351-360.

GODDEN, D.R. and BADDELEY, A.D. (1975) Context-dependent memory in two natural environments: on land and in water. *British Journal of Psychology*, 65, 325-331.

HEBB, D.O. (1949) *The Organisation of Behaviour*. New York: Wiley.

HUNTER, I.M.L. (1957) *Memory*. Harmondsworth: Penguin.

JAMES, W. (1890) *Talks to Teachers on Psychology, and to Students on Some of Life's Ideals*. New York: Henry Holt.

KANDEL, E.R. and SCHWARTZ, J.H. (1982) Molecular biology of learning: Modulation of transmitter release. *Science*, 218, 433-443.

LANDAUER, T.K. (1986) How much do people remember? Some estimates of the quantity of learned information in long-term memory. *Cognitive Science*, 10, 477-492.

LASHLEY, K.S. (1950) In search of the engram. In *Symposium of the Society for Experimental Biology*, Vol. 4. New York: Cambridge University Press.

LOFTUS, E.F. (1979) *Eye Witness Testimony*. Harvard University Press.

LOFTUS, E.F. (1979) *Eye Witness Testimony*. Harvard University Press.

LOFTUS, E.F. and BURNS, T.E. (1982) Mental shock can produce retrograde amnesia. *Memory and Cognition*, 10, 319-323.

LOFTUS, E.F., LOFTUS, G.R. and MESSO, J. (1987) Some facts about 'weapon focus'. *Law and Human Behaviour*, 11, 55-62.

MANDLER, G. (1968) Organisatin and memory. In K.W. Spence and J.T. Spence (Eds.), *The Psychology of Learning and Motivation*, Vol. 2. New York: Academic Press.

MILLER, G.A. (1956) The magical number seven, plus or minus two: Some limits on our capacity for processing information. *Psychological Review*, 63, 81-97.

MISHKIN, M.S. and APPENZELLER, T. (1987) The anatomy of memory. *Scientific American*, 80-89.

MORGAN J.J.B. and LOVELL, G.D. (1928) *The Psychology of Abnormal People*. Harlow: Longman.

MORRIS, N. and JONES, D.M. (1990) Memory updating in the working memory: The role of the central executive. *British Journal of Psychology*, 81, 111-121.

MURDOCK, B.B. Jr. (1962) The serial position effect in free recall. *Journal of Experimental Psychology*, 64, 482-488.

PETERSON, L.R. and PETERSON, M.J. (1959) Short-term retention of individual items. *Journal of Experimental Psychology*, 58, 193-198.

SNYDER, M. and URANOWITZ, S.W. (1978) Reconstructing the past: Some cognitive consequences of person perception. *Journal of Personality and Social Psychology*, 36, 940-950.

SPERLING, G. (1960) The information available in brief visual presentations. *Psychological Monographs*, 74, No 489.

THOMAS, E.L. and ROBINSON, H.A. (1983) *Improving Reading in Every Class*. Needham Heights, MA: Allyn & Bacon.

TULVING, E. (1962) Subjective organisation in free-recall of unrelated words. *Psychological Review*, 69, 344-354.

TULVING, E. and PEARLSTONE, Z. (1966) Availability versus accessibility of information in memory for words. *Journal of Verbal Learning and Verbal Behaviour*, 5, 381-391.

TULVING, E. and THOMSON, D.M. (1973) Encoding specificity and retrieval process in episodic memory. *Psychological Review*, 80, 353-373.

UNDERWOOD, B.J. (1957) Interference and forgetting. *Psychological Review*, 64, 49-60.

WAUGH, N.C. and NORMAN, D.A. (1965) Primary Memory. *Psychological Review*, 72, 89-104.

YARNELL, P.R. and LYNCH, S. (1970) Retrograde memory immediately after concussion. *Lancet*, 1, 863-865.

ZECHMEISTER and NYBERG (1982) As cited in Gross, R.D. (1987) *Psychology: The science of mind and behaviour*, p. 169. London: Hodder & Stoughton.

GLOSSARY [Terms in bold type also appear as a separate entry]

Abreaction: a psychoanalytic term involving the release of emotional tension.

Amnestic (or amnesic) syndrome: is a clinical term for loss of LTM when there is no intellectual impairment, nor clouding of consciousness.

Amygdala: one area of the brain often found damaged in amnesics. It seems to be associated with processing new information.

Anterograde amnesia: is a memory problem involving an inability to remember new information, following brain trauma, with little damage to previous memories.

Attention: is a general term for all the processes by which we perceive selectively.

Catharsis: a psychoanalytic term meaning an emotional release.

Chunking: a process of organizing information which allows a number of items to be viewed as a single unit; e.g. the digits 1 9 8 7 could be viewed as four units or as a date, 1987, which is a single unit of information.

Confabulation: is when we fill in or create appropriate details to replace items we cannot recall.

Consolidation (prevention of): for a memory to be established, a period of time is needed for the changes in the nervous system, which are the result of learning, to occur. If this period is interrupted, say by a blow to the head, the memory will be impaired.

Context-dependent memory: the tendency to recall information more effectively when in the same context (e.g. the same room) as that in which the information was originally learned.

Context re-creation: this is a memory aid which works by re-creating the context (e.g. the location of learning) to support recall.

Displacement: occurs when the capacity of STM (7±2) is overloaded. Items will be lost from memory. (See also *serial position effect*.)

Echoic memory: is the brief sensory memory of auditory stimuli. Even if attention is elsewhere sounds or words can be recalled within 3 or 4 seconds.

Elaborative rehearsal: material is actively reorganized and elaborated while being held in STM. It is more beneficial than *maintenance rehearsal*.

ECT: (electroconvulsive therapy) is shock treatment in which a brief electric current is passed through the brain. It may be used in the treatment of severe depression.

Encoding: is the means by which information is put into your memory system. It may be acoustic (involving rehearsal in your head) or visual or semantic (by meaning).

Hippocampus: one of the areas of the brain often found damaged in amnesics. It seems to be associated with processing new information.

Iconic memory: is a brief sensory memory of visual information, lasting only a second or two.

Interference: what takes place between learning and recall can inhibit memory from being effective.

Levels of processing model: a model of how memory works that relates how long a memory lasts to how deeply it is processed (considering the *meaning* of a word requires deeper processing than judging whether it is written in capitals or lower case letters).

Long-term memory: a memory system which keeps memories for relatively long periods. It has a very large (some say unlimited) capacity. Items are stored in a relatively organized form.

Maintenance rehearsal: refers to the rehearsal which keeps information in STM. In contrast with *elaborative rehearsal* it gives little benefit.

Memory: the retention of experience or learning.

Mnemonic devices: these are ways of assisting memory by artificial devices, many of which depend for their success on visual imagery. They include method of loci, numeric pegword system, keyword method, narrative link and rhymes and rhythms.

Model: is a way of representing observed behaviour in a graphic form. Models usually result in further research to verify or challenge assumptions contained within them.

Neurotransmitters: chemicals that cross the synaptic cleft from one neuron to another and either excite or inhibit the adjacent neuron.

Organization: in order to maximize the effectiveness of long-term memory organization of information to be stored is essential. Sometimes an organizational hierarchy may be employed. This is a kind of tree diagram where narrower categories are subsumed under broader ones.

Perception: refers to the way we organize and interpret information received through the senses which enables us to recognize meaningful objects and events.

PQRST method: is a study skills technique: Preview, Question, Read, Self-recite and Test. This requires *organization* and *rehearsal* of material both of which assist long-term memory.

Primacy effect: is observed when the first few items of a list, in free recall, are remembered with greater accuracy than the middle items. (See also *recency effect*.)

Psychogenic amnesia: is the loss of memory for personal information which seems to stem from a stressful episode.

Recall: is the production of some information from memory. There may be few or no cues to assist in this active search.

Recency effect: can be seen when, in free recall, the last few items in a list (i.e. those most recently learned) are more frequently remembered than those in the middle. (See also *primacy effect*.)

Recognition: occurs when someone or something seems familiar to you, regardless of whether you can name or identify them.

Reconstructive memory: is the memory involved in rumours, for example. When passing on information the objective truth may be distorted by your own stereotypes, beliefs etc.

Redintegration: occurs when an item brings back many memories associated with a particular time or place. Photos lead us to redintegrate memories.

Rehearsal: this is a means of keeping information active. Maintenance rehearsal merely keeps things in short-term memory (e.g. telephone numbers). Elaborative rehearsal imposes organization and elaboration on material for long-term memory store.

Relearning: involves learning something which appeared to have been forgotten, for a second time. The relearning appears easier than the original learning.

Repression: a psychoanalytic term for a memory which is so painful that it is pushed into the unconscious. A repressed memory can only be accessed through therapy.

Retrieval: is the process of searching for information stored in memory, and finding it. Information not retrieved may be not *accessible* rather than not *available*.

Retrograde amnesia: after head injury a patient loses memory for some period of time prior to the injury.

Sensory register: is the system of holding information for a second or two, in an unprocessed, sensory form, e.g. an echo in your head of the last words someone spoke.

Serial position effect/curve: refers to our tendency to remember the first and last items in a list. The curve visually represents this tendency.

Short-term memory: is the memory system that keeps information for short periods of time only. Its capacity is limited to 7 ± 2 chunks of information. Material stored here is in a relatively unprocessed form.

State-dependent memory: recall is best when you are in the same emotional or physiological state as you were in when the information was learned.

Stereotypes: preconceived beliefs about people, places or objects, held even in the face of logical disproof.

Storage: is the retention of encoded material.

Temporal lobe: there is one temporal lobe in each cerebral hemisphere. Damage here may lead to memory loss.

Trace decay: the theory that learning leaves a trace in the brain as a result of nerve cell excitation and that this trace fades over time.

Tulving and Thomson's encoding specificity principle: retrieval is most likely to occur if the cues at the time of recall match those at the time of encoding.

Two-process model: is a simple model to explain how the different memory systems might work together: the *sensory register* feeding into *short-term memory* where after *rehearsal* information may be transferred into *long-term memory*. Information can be 'lost' at any of these stages.

Weapon focus: refers to the tendency of people witnessing a crime involving the use of a weapon to concentrate their attention on the weapon.

Working memory model: is a more complex model than the *two process model* and *levels of processing model*. It replaces the passive STM store with a more active working memory system. A central executive controls the other components: the articulatory loop (inner voice) and the visuo-spatial scratch pad (inner eye). This model is still being developed.

ANSWERS TO SELF-ASSESSMENT QUESTIONS

SAQ 1 Select any two of the following with appropriate examples:

    (a) acoustic coding e.g. telephone numbers

    (b) visual coding e.g. a friend's face

    (c) semantic coding e.g. Every good boy deserves favour (EGBDF) and FACE for the notes of the treble clef.

SAQ 2 (a) chunking — grouping information into no more than 7 ± 2 chunks

    (b) organization — grouping the information with information of similar characteristics e.g. breeds of dog.

SAQ 3 — Meeting the friend and recognizing her = RECOGNITION.

    — Showing the photos = REDINTEGRATION.

    — Talking about the mutual friend = RECONSTRUCTIVE MEMORY.

    — Reminising over the party = could involve RECON-STRUCTIVE MEMORY; CONFABULATION; or perhaps even STATE/CONTEXT-DEPENDENT MEMORY.

SAQ 4 An item enters through the sensory modes. If it is not attended to, it is lost. If an item is attended to, it will pass into STM where it will be rehearsed, and information about it transferred to LTM, where it becomes a more permanent memory. If rehearsal ceases in STM, the item will be displaced by new, incoming items. An item can be lost from LTM by interference, decay, etc.

SAQ 5 (a) Phonetic

    (b) Semantic

    (c) Structural

    (d) Phonetic

    (e) Semantic

SAQ 6 Thinking of a rhyme does not require processing at the semantic level, only on the phonetic level, therefore the processing is shallow. Thinking of an adjective requires the semantic level of processing (i.e. deep processing) and so you should find that you recalled more of the adjective words than the rhyme words.

SAQ 7 (a) Central executive, articulatory loop, possibly visuo-spatial scratch pad.

    (b) Probably all four components.

    (c) Central executive, primary acoustic store, central executive, and possibly, articulatory loop.

SAQ 8 A signal is passed from one neuron to the next by means of a neurotransmitter, or chemical messenger. The neuro-transmitter is passed across the synaptic cleft. Some psychologists suggest that this excitation forms the basis of the memory trace which makes up STM. LTM results from neurological change.

SAQ 9 (a) Context re-creation.

    (b) Method of loci; numeric pegword system or narrative link.

    (c) Organization and/or PQRST method.

    (d) Keyword method.

SAQ 10 If material is not encoded or stored it cannot be available to memory. This relates to STM mainly. Accessibility is an LTM issue — how can memories be retrieved.

Theories of forgetting that concern accessibility:

    (1) Prevention of consolidation

    (2) Stereotypes

    (3) Repression

    (4) State/context-dependent forgetting.

SAQ 11 Possible causes of clinical amnesia:

    — damage to the brain (accidental/stroke)

    — alcoholism

    — ECT

    — ageing and senile dementia

    — encephalitis

    — brain surgery.